Stefan Czarnecki

Write Like Your Hands are on Fire
50 Dynamic Writing Prompts and How to Teach Them

© Lingolino™ Publishing, Schwarzenberg

Credits

Title	Write like Your Hands Are on Fire
	50 Dynamic Writing Prompts and How to Teach Them
Author	Stefan Czarnecki
Illustrations	Barbara Capri and Stefan Czarnecki for Lingolino™
Acknowledgements	Many thanks to Alice Czarnecki, Kirsten Peterson and Steve Crowley for reading and revising my prompts and for offering valuable advice.
ISBN	ISBN 978-3-8334-9889-3
Printed by	Books on Demand GmbH, Norderstedt
Copyright	© 2007, 1. Edition
	Lingolino™ and the author, Stefan Czarnecki

Lingolino™ Publishing
Dickach 87, A-6867 Schwarzenberg, AUSTRIA
info@lingolino.com, www.lingolino.com

for Valentina

"Whatever your mind can conceive, you can achieve"

Contents

Introduction

Why Teach Writing?

Like many other skills that a child learns or acquires during a lifetime, becoming a capable writer requires practice and guidance. By encouraging and teaching children to become emergent writers, you are expanding their ability to communicate ideas and influence others. Through writing, you are enhancing the child's capability to communicate, entertain, inform, persuade and change the world.

I have written this book to inspire teachers to bring joy to language learning, by making writing easier and more joyful for you to teach, and, more importantly, I have written it to help you convey to your students, that writing is a joyful and purposeful life skill.

Write Like Your Hands Are on Fire!

This book can be used to spark short writing activities or to ignite long-term writing projects, like a Young Author's Project.

When I first presented the "Back to the Future" prompt (Prompt 9) to my students, we were having a writing festival at our school. I had asked a student to come in a day before the festival. This student was especially talented at arts & crafts and I gave him some material (an old shoe box, glue, tape, markers, etc.) and asked him: "Do you think you can build a time machine out of this?" The student was eager and thrilled and, in about twenty-five minutes, he came up with a contraption which looked quite intimidating. I was reluctant to play with the dials!

The next day, I had strapped the contraption onto a chair. When the students came into class, I sat on the chair and turned some dials. "And now kids, I am going to send myself into the past!" I explained.

The students were very excited and immediately after that, I explained what we would be doing: "We are going to invent a time machine!"

I showed them an excerpt from Steven Spielberg's *Back to the Future*, when Doc Brown explains how the time machine works and when Marty uses it the first time. After that, I could hardly hold the students back anymore. I told them that on their sheet of paper, they should draw their time machine and explain how it works. The children's' hands were moving so fast, they looked like they were on fire!

I had succeeded in withdrawing the kids from the real world! They were writing like their hands were on fire, even the most reluctant ones!

Topic

When I started to write this book, I asked colleagues what they looked for most in a writing prompt. One of the comments that kept coming up was that they wanted a prompt that was comprehensible and does not demand specialized knowledge. In other words, the topics should be immediate to the students and not abstract or vague. For this reason, I have tried to construct the writing prompts in this book in a way to spark ideas, thoughts and feelings in the mind of the writer. The prompts are all linked to social, historical and cultural events.

Pre-Writing Tasks

Before your students start writing, it is important to set the atmosphere. Writing should be taught with emotion and fire and it is essential to stimulate young writers right from the beginning. Kids love to hear exciting and hard-to-believe facts and figures about their writing topic like "Did you know that Evil Knievel tried to break a world record by jumping over 13 Pepsi delivery trucks with his motorcycle? He came down wheel-first and ended up breaking his collarbone, right arm and both legs!" Now, asking your students to write a story about something crazy that they once did (See prompt 23) should be effortless.

Making Sense of the Topic

Young writers need background information about their writing topic so the task does not seem ambiguous or abstract. If you are using a prompt about Martin Luther King, tell the students who he was and read "I Have a Dream" to them so that they are able to make connections between the topic and the task.

Brainstorming

Begin by writing the topic on the board and ask the students what things come to mind. Sometimes I even take the time to write the words into categories (nouns, verbs, adjectives).

Task

When reading the task to the students, I ask them to close their eyes. I read the task and ask them to imagine that they are in this particular situation. I ask: "Do you see it?", "Do you smell it?", and "Can you feel it?" The students answer with their eyes closed and I continue writing words on the board. Then, I read the prompt again and ask the students to open their eyes. "What other things come to mind?" I keep writing until the board is full. Then I tell the students that it is their turn to write.

Starters

One of the hardest things for kids to do in writing is getting started. Even if they have a topic and a task, they still struggle with how to start their story. The trick is to give the kids suggestions without writing the story for them.

Before reading the suggestions in the "Starters" section, ask your students to give suggestions on how to start their stories. Then, read the different "Starters" to them. By now, the children should really be excited to get going and this is exactly where you want them.

Guidance

Let your students start writing. A good way to start is to have them draw a picture of the main character and describe the picture. Another way to start is to have the children use the "Story Sequence" template in the back of this book and write a summary of what will happen. After they are finished, they can add details. As the children are writing, read some of the guiding questions to them: "Talk about where you are!", "Write down what you feel!"

Word Box

The word box is to give the students a chance to expand, enhance and play with vocabulary. Talk about the words in the box. Ask the children what the words mean. How could they relate to the story? Get the students to write as much as they can, without being distracted. They should try to use some of the vocabulary in this box. I don't require that they use dictionaries at this point. They can be used later. If students are stuck because they don't know a word or how to write a word, tell them – write it on the board for them – just keep them writing.

Peer Editing

One of the strongest tools in writing is peer editing. Even as adults, we want to know what other people think. If you have a small group, have each student read their story to the class. While the children are listening, they can write feedback and suggestions on post-its notes or small pieces of paper. Then, have the class give oral feedback on which parts of the story were good and which parts need improvement. If your class is bigger, put the students into editing groups and have them read their stories to the group.

Re-Writing Process

Once the students get their work back, they should add information and details where needed by answering the questions on the post-it notes. Then they are ready to present their second draft to the class for peer editing.

Draft 2

At his stage of the writing process, I collect student work and help them to enhance their writing by adding details. I do not correct spelling or grammar yet. It is helpful to put small post-it notes on the pages, asking questions which, after they are answered, give more detail to the story: "What does this feel like?", Why did you do this?", What was the weather like?"

Mini-Lessons

If you notice a general area for improvement in many of the stories, throw in mini-lessons on grammar, spelling or writing style where needed. Have all the children go back and self-edit their work with regards to your mini-lesson.

Self-Corrections	Before correcting, give the students a copy of the "Writing Checklist" hereinafter, have them look for capitalization, spelling and other common mistakes. They should then check off each rubric when they have finished the relevant area.
Correcting Student Work	When correcting creative writing, keep in mind that this work comes from the heart. Refrain from negative comments and remarks. If the writing is messy, tell the students to do their best when writing a good copy. If there are a lot of grammar and spelling mistakes, use this as an initiative to throw in an extra grammar or spelling lesson.
Presenting Your Work	One of the essential aspects of writing is celebrating and acknowledging the students' hard work. The section *Presenting Your Work* gives suggestions on how students can present their final drafts.
Sample Lessons	The lesson plans section of this book gives a clear and detailed outline of how to use this book when teaching writing.
Assessment	The "Score Your Writing" rubric helps teachers and students asses the writing process. The rubric is child friendly and should first be filled out by the student and then by the teacher, followed by a short discussion.

Writing Genres in this Book

Overview

The writing genres in this book have been indexed on pages 11-14. The goal is to give you a quick overview of which prompts can be used to teach or support which genres. The following genres are used in this book:

Autobiographical

An autobiography is a person's story, written by that person.

Biographical

Biographies are written stories of a person's life that were written by someone else.

Descriptive writing

The goal of this genre is to describe a person, place or thing in vivid detail.

Expository writing

The goal of this genre is to give information such as an explanation or directions.

Narrative writing

The goal of this genre is to tell a story of an experience, event, or sequence of events while holding the reader's interest.

Persuasive writing

The goal of this genre is to give an opinion in an attempt to convince the reader that this point of view is valid.

Prompts in this Book

26	Autobiography	*Non-Fiction* Write an autobiography	Autobiographical	40
27	The Best School Day Ever	*Fiction* Write about the best school day you ever had or about what would make a perfect school day for you	Narrative	41
28	Roswell	*Fantasy, Science Fiction* You are witness to a UFO sighting	Narrative	42
29	Nostradamus	*Fantasy* Make a prophecy. Write about the future	Narrative	43
30	Mountain Madness	*Adventure* If you were to go on an exciting exhibition, where would you go?	Narrative	44
31	Sweet Sixteen	*Fiction* Write about your most outrageous birthday party	Narrative	45
32	The Good Samaritan	*Fiction, Parable* Would you act as a good Samaritan?	Narrative	46
33	Whodunit?	*Mystery, Detective* Write a Whodunit	Narrative	47
34	Nineteen-Eighty-Four	*Literature, Science Fiction* What would life be like in George Orwell's world?	Narrative	48
35	Domestic Robot	*Science, Technology* You have invented a robot to help you with your every-day life	Descriptive, Expository, Narrative	49
36	Different Places, Different Faces	*Travel* The most interesting place I ever visited	Narrative, Autobiographical	50
37	How the Elephant Got Its Wrinkles	*Fantasy, Fiction* How did the elephant get its wrinkles?	Narrative	51
38	Indiana Jones	*Adventure, Fantasy* You are looking for a long, lost artifact	Narrative	52

MONSter for sale

Topic

Classified advertising is a form of advertising which is particularly common in newspapers and magazines. Classified advertising usually consists of a short text about an item being sold and a telephone number to call for more information.

Task

While reading the newspaper, you stumble across the following classified ad: *Spine-chilling monster needs a loving new home. Already housebroken, extremely intelligent, very playful and needs a lot of attention. He is over eight feet tall and he will follow your every command. Please contact me for more information!*

You react to this ad and now have a scary, eight-foot monster at home that will follow your every command. What do you do with it?

Starters

Describe the excitement when the postman brings your monster in a box.

Guidance

- Describe your monster.
- Where do you take your monster and what happens there?
- Are people scared of it?

Word Box

horrifying, terrifying, creepy, daunting, bulky, hefty, enormous, foul-smelling, compassionate, benevolent, despicable, dreadful, repulsive, stomach-turning

Presenting Your Work

Make a scary mask which best suits the description of your monster. Wear the mask when you present your story.

2   a Midsummer Night's Dream

Topic

A Midsummer Night's Dream is a play written by William Shakespeare in the late 1500's. In the play, Hermia loves Lysander and Helena loves Demetrius, but the mischievous hobgoblin Puck uses a magic potion that makes the wrong men love the wrong women. Even Titania, the fairy queen, is made to fall in love with a workman with the head of a donkey!

Task

You are the hobgoblin Puck. You have just created a new potion. Describe the potion you have invented and what you will use it for.

Starters

- Describe the setting (are you in a small, dark cave, like that of a Hobbit?
- Describe where your finished potion is standing. Perhaps it is on an old, crooked table, bubbling out of the neck of the glass?

Guidance

- What does your potion look and smell like?
- Where do you keep it?
- What can it be used for?
- Describe when, why and how you will use the potion.

Word Box

potion, mixture, brew, transform, change, bubbles, suds, bottle, froth, drink, slurp, swig, love struck, infatuated, mad, foolish, witty, droll, bubbly, fizzy

Presenting Your Work

Roll up your piece of writing, tie a ribbon around it and stick it in an old, clean olive-oil bottle. Then, put a cork on the bottle so it looks like the recipe of a secret potion!

The New Planet That Never Was

Topic	In 1860, the French Mathematician, Urbain Le Verrier, announced that a new planet, Vulcan, existed in an orbit between Mercury and the Sun. Soon after, many other scientists, mostly amateurs, claimed to have seen the planet. Despite many years of searching, Vulcan was never officially seen or found. The name was however given to the fictional home of Mr. Spock in Star Trek.
Task	You are a scientist and have just discovered a new planet. In a diary entry, write about your discovery.
Starters	• Describe the setting.
	• Are you sitting in your room with a telescope, looking at the stars and you accidentally see a planet?
	• Perhaps you are in a big observatory and have been looking for a new planet for years?
	• Describe the excitement of finally reaching your goal.
Guidance	• Where is the planet?
	• What does it look like?
	• Who or what lives on the planet?
Word Box	discover, notice, uncover, remote, distant, outlying, isolated, galaxy, solar system, universe, deep space, cosmos, dazzling, intelligent life, milky way
Presenting Your Work	Market your planet! Make posters starting a marketing campaign, selling trips to your new planet.

David Copperfield

Topic

The magician David Copperfield was born in Metuchen, New Jersey. At the age of twelve, he became the youngest person ever to be admitted to the Society of American Magicians. David Copperfield has been called "The Master of Grand Illusion." His magic shows have aired in over forty countries and have been seen by an estimated three billion people.

Task

You are the "Master of Grande Illusion." You are performing your new illusion or magic trick in front of a sell out crowd. Describe your illusion and what happens as you perform it.

Starters

- It was a sell out crowd! My name was on the billboard outside …
- The lights went out and smoke rose from under the curtains …

Guidance

- What is it like to be presenting your illusion for the first time?
- As you peak through the curtains before the show, what do you see?
- Describe your illusion or trick and how the crowd reacts to it.
- Does everything run smoothly?

Word Box

illusion, fantasy, figment of your imagination, deception, mislead, fool, exciting, disappear, vanish, fade, appear, emerge, come to light, trick

Presenting Your Work

Use craft paper, tin foil, stars, and other craft material to make your text look magical. Writing your text on black craft paper with a white or yellow pencil crayon is excellent for this!

DEEP-SEA Explorer

Topic

Jacques Cousteau was one of the most famous underwater explorers that ever lived. Cousteau's boat was called the Calypso, and with it, he experienced more than a great adventure. The Frenchman also helped invent the jet-propelled submarine.

Task

Cousteau has just helped to invent the jet-propelled submarine and has asked you to be the first to use it. Write about your experiences in a log book entry.

Starters

You are on the telephone and have just found out that you will be the first person to pilot the jet-propelled submarine…

Guidance

- What is it like to be chosen to be the first person to pilot the submarine?
- What does it feel like to be in the submarine?
- What does it feel like to be lowered into the water?
- What things do you see underwater?
- Are there any dangers?

Word Box

eager, thrilled, energized, anxious, uneasy, restless, fearful, proud, pompous, swollen with pride, successful, amazed, flabbergasted, gobsmacked, stunned

Presenting Your Work

Make a model of your trip and your discoveries out of an empty shoe box. You can put anything inside that you may have seen or used on your trip: a submarine, fish, sharks, plants or a terrifying creature.

Superheroes

Topic

In June 1938, after years of trying and being rejected, Jerry Siegel and Joe Shuster finally had their creation, Superman, published in Action Comics. The "Man of Steel" possessed many super-human powers, like being able to fly, having super-human strength, and having x-ray vision. That first issue of Superman is now worth $440,000!

Task

Create and describe your own superhero (or) Create a villain with super powers.

Starters

- Describe your hero's (or) villain's arrival on earth.
- Where does he/she land?
- What does he think of "earthlings"?

Guidance

- Where does he/she come from?
- What does he/she look like?
- What special powers does he/she have?
- What weaknesses does he/she have?
- Why did he/she choose good over evil (or) evil over good?

Word Box

super-human, power, force, vigour, swift, high-speed, vigorous, mighty, robust, good, evil, phenomenal, extraordinary, ready to lend a hand, justice

Presenting Your Work

Make a life-size model of your super-hero or villain out of cardboard. Then, display your story beside the model.

Moby Dick

Topic

Moby-Dick is a novel that was written by Herman Melville in 1851. The novel describes the voyage of Captain Ahab on his whaling ship "The Pequod". Captain Ahab leads his crew on a hunt for a great whale, Moby-Dick. The journey comes to a dramatic and tragic peak when the crew catches sight of Moby-Dick. For three days, they battle with the white whale until Moby-Dick finally charges the ship itself.

Task

You are Ahab, the Captain of The Pequod. Write about your experiences as you and your crew battle against Moby Dick.

Starters

Describe your first day at sea, when you come out of your cabin, go on deck and head out to find the whale.

Guidance

- What does Moby Dick look like?
- What do you feel the first time you see him?
- What do you smell in the air as he approaches your ship?
- What does it feel like to be battling against the whale for three long days?
- Where in your body do you feel tired?
- What happens after Moby Dick charges your ship?

Word Box

journey, expedition, danger, hazard, threat, immense, enormous, vast, mighty, robust, resilient, intense, sore, hurting, throbbing, exhausted, drained

Presenting Your Work

Make an old diary to write down your experiences. Wear the edges and tear some pages out. Make it look old and worn.

ROBINSON CRUSOE

Topic

Robinson Crusoe is a novel written by Daniel Defoe in 1719. The book is about an English castaway who spends 28 years on a remote island, encountering many adventures before finally being rescued.

Task

Your ship is caught in a fierce storm and sinks. You manage to hold on to a wooden door in the water and eventually manage to make it to shore. You don't know if anybody else made it. Write down your experiences as you first reach the shore.

Starters

Close your eyes and imagine yourself lying on the shore of a beautiful, white, sandy beach. You slowly open your eyes and the sun blinds you. Then you remember what happened …

Guidance

- What is going through your head?
- What are your first thoughts?
- What do you do first after you have recovered from the strenuous events?
- Describe how it is ironic to be in such a beautiful yet threatening place.

Word Box

storm, tempest, rough, rigid, chilly, murky, gloomy, threatening, deafening, thunderous, splatter, scorching, sizzling, blistering, isolated, deserted, cut off

Presenting Your Work

Make a treasure chest. Write your text on a scroll and tie a ribbon around it. Then, store your scroll in the chest.

Back to the Future

Topic	In 1985, Amblin Entertainment released the movie *Back to the Future*. The movie is about a crazy scientist, Doc Brown, who makes a time machine out of a fancy sports car. Doc's young friend Marty McFly, a typical American teenager, is accidentally sent back to 1955 and has to find a way to get back home.
Task	You are a mad scientist who has just invented a time machine. Describe your time machine and the first time you use it.
Starters	• You are sitting in your time machine. Describe all the gadgets. • What do they look like and what can they be used for?
Guidance	• What does your time machine look like? • What is special about it? • How does it work? • Where do you go on your first trip? • Which famous person would you visit? Why? • What questions would you ask him/her?
Word Box	time-travel, era, period, hyperspace, past, yesteryear, forthcoming, future, eager, wound-up, swift, like a flash, astounded, stunned, Milky Way, universe
Presenting Your Work	Build a model of your time machine out of card board or other material. Save a space on it to present your work.

Famous architect

Topic

The famous architect Frank Lloyd Wright was born in Wisconsin in 1867. Wright was especially well known for designing the Guggenheim Museum in New York. Unfortunately, Wright died shortly before the completion of the project. Wright lived in an amazing house called "Fallingwater", which was built over a waterfall.

Task

Write about your dream house.

Starters

- I would love to live in...
- I see myself living in...

Guidance

- Where would you most like to live and why?
- What kind of building would you like to live in?
- What does the building look like?
- What do the rooms look like and how are they furnished?

Word Box

house, home, dwelling, building, bungalow, cottage, mansion, flat, farmhouse, country, city, villa, studio, seaside, mountainside, lodge, manor

Presenting Your Work

Draw blueprints of your dream house. Draw the blueprints to scale and on transparent paper.

Rocket in Your Backyard

Topic

The history of modern rocketry was born when the scientist Robert Goddard invented the world's first liquid fuelled rocket engine. Goddard launched the first liquid-fuelled rocket in 1926 at his Aunt Effie's farm in Auburn, Massachusetts. The first flight, which lasted just 2.5 seconds, landed in a cabbage field.

Task

You and a friend have built a rocket in your backyard. In the afternoons you sit inside it to play. One day, while you are sitting inside, you suddenly hear a loud blast …

Starters

- Describe what you are doing in the rocket before you hear the blast.
- Perhaps you are playing cards?
- What happens to your game when you hear the blast?

Guidance

- What was the blast?
- What has happened?
- Is the rocket moving?
- Has somebody or something crashed against it?
- Where is it heading?

Word Box

sky-rocket, soar, shoot up, through the roof, rise, go sky-high, startled, worried, troubled, clasp, seize, cling to, stare, gawk, shriek, squeal, scream

Presenting Your Work

Build a model rocket out of an empty plastic bottle or paper maché. Put your story into the rocket.

Rock around the Clock

12

Topic	In 1957, John Lennon formed a legendary rock band in Liverpool, England, that would change music forever. The Beatles: John, Paul, Ringo and George, were one of the most successful bands of all times, selling over 1.3 billion records, tapes and CD's worldwide! The Beatles had 22 Nr.1 singles in the U.S. alone!
Task	Write a text about your favourite musician(s). It can be a singer, a band, a classical or rock musician, anything you like.

Starters

- Ever since I can remember, I have loved …
- Let me tell you about …

Guidance

- Where does the singer/band come from?
- Describe what the singer or band members look like.
- What kind of music is it?
- What makes the music so special?
- What is your favourite song?
- Are there lyrics to a song of this artist that you especially like? Why?
- What do your parents say when you are listening to this music?

Word Box

absolutely, downright, outstanding, exceptional, first-rate, superb, deafening, ear-splitting, legendary, famous, prominent, well-known, celebrity, superstar

Presenting Your Work

Use an overhead or CD marker and write your text on a blank CD.

I Have a Dream

Topic

On April 16, 1963, Martin Luther King wrote his famous *Letter from Birmingham City Jail*, in which he states that "Injustice anywhere is a threat to justice everywhere." He also wrote a famous civil rights speech entitled *I Have a Dream* in which he expresses the dreams and aspirations he has for a better world.

Task

Write your own speech entitled "I Have a Dream." In it, write about the dreams and hopes you have for a better world.

Starters

Start out just like Martin Luther King: "I have a dream that one day …"

Guidance

- Read or watch the speech "I Have a Dream" by Martin Luther King (You can find it on the internet)
- What things need to be changed in today's world? (Racism, the environment, terrorism, …)
- What is your dream for mankind?

Word Box

affectionate, considerate, compassionate, equal, tolerant, appreciative, prejudice, discrimination, intolerance, open-minded, unprejudiced, racism

Presenting Your Work

Write your speech on a scroll and present it to your class. Present your speech with passion!

Peer Pressure

Topic

Peer pressure means changing your behaviour, because you want to belong to a group. Peer pressure can be observed mainly amongst teenagers, who smoke or drink for example, because their friends do it.

Task

There is a youth gang in your neighbourhood that you really want to join. The leader of the gang has an initiation task for you that you think is dangerous. You really want to belong to the group. What do you do?

Story Starters

Describe the setting. Where does the gang meet?

Guidance

- Describe the members of the gang.
- What are their names?
- What do they look like?
- What do they act like?
- Who is the leader?
- What is the initiation?
- How do you react?
- How do the members of the gang react to your decision?

Word Box

pressure, not allowed, difficult, scared, fear, angry, confused, smoking, drinking, dangerous, hazardous, crazy, impossible, shack, shed, gang, band

Presenting Your Work

Write your story on long strips of cardboard and use the cardboard to build a tree-house in which your gang meets.

Christopher Columbus

Topic

On April 11, 1492, Christopher Columbus signed a contract with Spain, which granted him funds to sail to Asia to get spices. Soon after, on August 3, 1492, Columbus departed from Palos, Spain with three ships: a large carrack, The Santa Maria, and two smaller caravels, The Nina and The Piñta.

Task

You are on board the Santa Maria. Write a letter to a family member about what you expect to find and see on your journey at sea.

Starters

Describe your walk to the harbor as you smell the ocean and see the mighty Santa Maria, busy with people.

Guidance

- What do you feel as the Santa Maria sets sail?
- Why did you decide to go on board the Santa Maria?
- What do you think you will experience on your journey?
- What things do you see while traveling?

Word Box

explorer, adventurer, sea, ocean, navigate, route, thrilling, quest, journey, expedition, exploration, voyage, anxious, timid, brave, bold, map, compass

Presenting Your Work

Cover your paper with Soya Sauce to make it look really old. You can also have someone help you to burn the edges. Then, write your letter on the old piece of paper and stick it in a bottle.

My Dark, Scary Basement

16

Help!

Topic	Everybody is afraid of something! Arachnophobia for example, is a fear of spiders. Children are often afraid of the dark, insects, spiders, bees, heights, water, snakes, dogs, birds, or other things.
Task	Describe the scariest place in the world.
Starters	The most challenging part of this task is using the right words and being able to describe the setting so your reader will get goose bumps!
Guidance	• Brainstorm and write down as many adjectives as you can that describe your scary place.
	• Think about what makes a place scary.
	• List many synonyms for 'scary'.
	• Write about your scary place.
	• What do you most dislike about being here or thinking of it?
	• Describe yourself going to your scary place.
	• How do you overcome your fear?
Word Box	scary, frightening, creepy, terrifying, daunting, forbidding, intimidating menacing, startling, fearsome, worrisome, goose bumps, hair-raising, chilling
Presenting Your Work	Make a display board. The board should resemble a dark forest. Out of card paper, cut out a scary, dark shape that resembles something in the forest, like a dark tree, a spider or a rock. Write your text on the card paper and put it on the bulletin board.

INVENT a Holiday

Topic

The word holiday comes from the words holy and day. Holidays originally represented special religious days. Today, the word is used to mean any special day of rest. A holiday can also be a day set aside by a country for celebration, like Independence Day.

Task

Christmas is celebrated on December 25th, February 14th is Valentine's Day and the second Sunday in May is Mother's Day. Create your own holiday! What is celebrated on this day and why?

Starters

December 25th is Christmas Day. It marks an annual holiday that celebrates the Birth of Christ ... (Apply this to your own holiday!)

Guidance

- What day is it?
- What are you celebrating?
- What customs are related to this holiday?
- What do people normally eat on this holiday?

Word Box

celebrate, rejoice, commemorate, remember, honour, festival, event, presents, gifts, offerings, decoration, ornaments, light, be merry, joyful, blissful, jubilant

Presenting Your Work

Make cards that celebrate your holiday. Send the card to family or friends. You can also have a folk-fest in your classroom, commemorating the new holidays you and your classmates created.

Family Fable

Topic

A fable is a short story in which animals are given human qualities, such as being able to speak. Usually, a fable ends with a moral or lesson to be learned. Often, fables give the reader a chance to laugh at human foolishness, by providing examples of behavior we should avoid.

Task

Write a fable about your family. All your family members are animals with human qualities. Give the reader a chance to laugh at something silly a family member does. Also, make sure you include a moral or lesson to be learned.

Starters

Think of a possible moral or lesson that you would like to base your story on.

Guidance

- Think about what kind of animal would suit which of your family members and why.
- Where do you think your family would live if you were animals?
- What human qualities do your family members have?
- Can they speak?
- Can they read?
- Think about an event in your life in which you learned a lesson. Base your fable on this.

Word Box

fable, tale, legend, moral, message, meaning, lesson, warning, caution, cautionary, forewarning, foolish, unwise, thoughtless, ridiculous, mad, odd

Presenting Your Work

Make a class folder of all the fables and take ten minutes every morning to read one fable and talk about the moral or message.

The Three (Nasty) Pigs and the (Good) Wolf

Topic

Everyone knows the fairy tale of the "Three little Pigs", in which Mother Pig sends her three little piglets out to make the strongest house for the family. The first little pig builds a house of straw, but a wolf blows it down and eats the pig. The second pig builds its house out of sticks and also gets eaten. The third pig builds its house out of brick, which the wolf can not blow down. The wolf tries to come down the chimney, but the pig sets up a pot of boiling water and eats the wolf.

Task

Rewrite this or any other fairy tale, making the good character(s) bad and the bad character(s) good.

Starters

Once upon a time there was a horrible, revolting pig, which sent her three wicked piglets out to steal a house from a wolf…

Guidance

- Brainstorm and write down as many awful and unpleasant words you can think of to describe your (good) character.
- Is there a moral in your new fairy tale?
- Use chants and phrases like "Little pig, little pig, let me in…"

Word Box

horrible, awful, hideous, evil, wicked, nasty, unpleasant, revolting, obnoxious, annoying, shrieking, screeching, sinister, creepy, gloomy, good, pleasant

Presenting Your Work

Make your book look like a classic fairy tale and draw illustrations for your text.

My Constitution

Topic	A national constitution is a document that outlines the rules and values that govern a country. A constitution describes the political principles, procedures, powers and duties of a government. Most national constitutions also guarantee rights to the people.
Task	Write your own constitution, outlining the powers, duties, chores, responsibilities, rights and privileges of all your family members. You can also write a constitution for your classroom.
Starters	I, _____ (name), in order to form an even more wonderful family, establish Justice, provide Rights, Privileges and Freedom for All, do establish this Constitution for the _____ (name) Family.
Guidance	• Article One establishes the political principles of our family (What we believe in). • Article Two establishes the political hierarchy of our family members, as well as their powers, duties, chores and responsibilities. • Article Three establishes the Fundamental Rights of every family member.
Word Box	creation, structure, organization, law, ruling, abide, tolerate, freedom, choice, independence, free will, restriction, control, limitation, restriction, democracy
Presenting Your Work	Write your constitution on a long scroll and present it. Put a wax seal on it and set a date where, in front of witnesses, you will officially sign it.

The MOVE

Topic

Immigration is the movement of people from one place to another. Canada has the highest immigration rate in the world. In 2004, almost 251,000 people immigrated to Canada from other countries around the world.

Task

Imagine you come home from school one day and your parents tell you that you are going to move to a new city or country. How do you react?

Starters

I came home from school one day thinking nothing out of the ordinary. Then, my dad sat the family down in the living room. He only did this when he had something important to say. He told us we were going to move…

Guidance

- What is your first reaction to having to move?
- What will you tell your friends?
- What is the place like that you live in now?
- What do you love about it?
- What do you imagine your new place to be like?
- Are you scared or anxious? Why?

Word Box

move, relocate, relocation, job, career, home, residence, home town, place of birth, fearful, anxious, timid, eager, keyed up, wound up, travel, moving truck

Presenting Your Work

Find a picture of your house and paste it on a piece of paper. Write your story underneath the picture.

HeNry ford

Topic

Henry Ford was born in the state of Michigan in 1863. In 1896, Ford built his first car. In 1902, he built another car, which was the fastest car of its time. Soon after, Ford cars were made on assembly lines to make cars cheaper and available to more people.

Task

Write about your dream car.

Starters

Begin with a sales slogan like "The _____ (name of your car) combines elegance, vigor and spirit. It moves like …

Guidance

- What does your dream car look like?
- What can it do?
- What kind of gadgets do you have inside and what can they be used for?
- Why is the car perfect for you?
- Write about a trip that you take in your dream car.

Word Box

stunning, striking, attractive, elegant, stylish, smart, sharp, fly, zip, zoom, dash, force, energy, mood, atmosphere, soul, unique, exclusive, sporty

Presenting Your Work

Make or draw a model of your dream car. Write the text on a piece of paper and store the text in the trunk or under the hood.

Evil Knievel

Topic

"Evil" Knievel, Jr., born October 17, 1938 in Butte, Montana, is an American stuntman, best known for his public displays of long distance, high-altitude motorcycle jumping which often resulted in serious injuries. Once, Evil Knievel tried to break a world record by jumping over 13 Pepsi delivery trucks with his motorcycle. He came down wheel-first and ended up breaking his collarbone, right arm and both legs!

Task

Write about something crazy or dangerous that happened to you or someone you know.

Starters

- When I was ____ years old, …
- I remember it like it was yesterday. I still feel a sharp pain in my right arm when I think of it…

Guidance

- Describe what you did and why was it dangerous?
- What happened to you?
- What did your friends or parents say?
- What lesson did you learn?

Word Box

crazy, wild, foolish, senseless, silly, extreme, outrageous, stunt, feat, spectacular act, record, dare, challenge, courage, risk, have the nerve

Presenting Your Work

Make a "Guinness World Record" certificate for yourself, commemorating your stunt. At the bottom, write the lesson you learned!

It's My Vote

Topic	The voting age of a country is the minimum age established by law that a person must reach, in order to be able to vote in a national election. In most countries, the legal voting age is 18. In some countries it is 16.
Task	Should children be able to vote? Write a short, argumentative paper on whether or not you think children should be able to vote.
Starters	Before you start, write down five reasons to back up your argument.
Guidance	• What is the legal voting age in your country? • Do you agree with the voting age in your country? • At what age do you think people should be able to vote? • Back up your opinion.
Word Box	vote, take part in an election, cast your vote, ballot, selection, politics, political beliefs, political views, opinion, poll, legal age, make your choice, democracy
Presenting Your Work	Make up a ballot sheet. Make two columns, one that is titled "yes" and one that is titled "no". The words "yes" and "no" should have circles beside them so that an "X" can be placed in it. Write your arguments in appropriate columns. Write your introduction above the columns.

The World's Most Famous Scientist

Topic

In 1928, the Scottish scientist Sir Alexander Fleming discovered penicillin. Penicillin refers to a group of antibiotics, which help fight bacteria infections in your body. The discovery of penicillin, which was found by chance, changed modern medicine.

Task

If you could invent or discover something, what would you hope to invent or discover and why?

Starters

Begin by writing about your discovery or invention.

Guidance

- Why did you decide to invent it?
- What did you feel when you found out that your discovery or invention worked?
- What is your invention or discovery used for?
- What does it look like?

Word Box

experiment, research, trial, conduct an experiment, result, findings, cure, heal, treat, treatment, medicine, medication, modern, technology, science

Presenting Your Work

Create a package insert or instruction manual for your invention or discovery.

autobiography

Topic	An autobiography is a story of a person's life, written by that person. Famous autobiographies include: *The Autobiography of Benjamin Franklin,* Helen Keller's *The Story of My Life* and Maya Angelou's *I Know Why the Caged Bird Sings.*
Task	Write an autobiography.
Starters	Make a timeline of your life, including significant events that happened to you and/or your family.
Guidance	• When and where were you born? • Who are your parents and what do they do? • Do you have siblings? • What are some exciting or interesting things that have happened in your life?
Word Box	life story, story of your life, account, chronicle, record, family, parents, grandparents, siblings, relatives, relations, ancestors, personal, kin, loved ones
Presenting Your Work	Make a family tree and include it in your autobiography. Make a book out of your autobiography and put a picture of yourself on the cover page.

The Best school Day Ever

Topic	Schools existed as far back as Greek times, if not earlier. Compulsory education is education that children are required to receive by law. Compulsory primary education was affirmed as a Human Right by the Universal Declaration of Human Rights in 1948.
Task	Write about the best school day you ever had. Alternatively, write about what your ideal school day would be like.
Starters	You arrive at school and your principal tells you that you are able to plan the whole day. What do you decide to do?
Guidance	• How does the day start? • What subjects do you have? • What do you have for a snack? • What makes this the best school day ever?
Word Box	school, teach, educate, class, lesson, period, grade, teacher, sports, coach, science, social studies, geography, history, literature, mathematics, language
Presenting Your Work	Make up a timetable of your ideal school day to go with your story. It can be a time table for a whole week as well!

  ROSWELL

Topic	In July, 1947, the Roswell Army Air Field issued a press release that they had recovered a crashed flying saucer. Soon after, the commanding General stated that it was only a hot-air balloon. Today, no one really knows what happened. The US military claims that it was a research balloon, but some people believe it was a UFO.
Task	You have witnessed a UFO sighting. Describe in detail what you saw.
Starters	You are looking out your bedroom window. You breathe in the fresh night air. Suddenly, you see something strange …
Guidance	• What do you see? • Is it bright? • Is it in the sky? • Does it look dangerous? • Do you go outside to have a look, or are you scared? • What happens next?
Word Box	UFO, unidentified flying object, flying saucer, spaceship, alien spacecraft, alien, unknown, unfamiliar, strange, extraterrestrial, Martian, creature
Presenting Your Work	Design the front page of a newspaper or magazine, Make a newspaper headline and draw pictures of what you saw that night. Include your story on the cover page of the newspaper.

Nostradamus

Topic

Nostradamus was a French apothecary, something like a modern day pharmacist. In 1555, Nostradamus published a book of prophecies for which he became famous. His book was a collection of future predictions, some of which are said to have become reality.

Task

Make up a prophecy. Write a short text about what you think life will be like 200 years from now.

Starters

I have just had the most wonderful/horrible vision …

Guidance

- What will the future be like?
- What will traffic be like?
- What will houses look like?
- What will school be like?
- How will people view the lifestyle we lead today?

Word Box

prophecy, prediction, guess, predict, anticipate, outlook, likely, hope, future, opportunity, prosperity, fortune, poverty, technology, possible, fortune, fate

Presenting Your Work

Record your text about the future on the computer by making an mp3 recording of it. After, burn it on a CD.

MOUNTAIN MADNESS

Topic

Scott Fischer was a famous mountain climber who reached the summit of Mount Everest in 1994. In May of 1996, Scott climbed Mount Everest for a second time with another group of climbers. The second climb turned out to be a horrible tragedy. Eight of the world's best climbers including Scott died during a savage storm. The well known story was made into an exciting book by Jon Krakauer called "Into Thin Air." Scott Fischer had a company called "Mountain Madness", which took people on exciting expeditions all over the world.

Task

If you were to go on an exciting expedition, where would you go? Write a story about your experiences.

Starters

Describe the place you want to go to and why. Research the area you want to visit and write about why this would be so exciting for you.

Guidance

- What country or place would you visit?
- What is exciting about this place?
- What is there to see and do?
- Write about your experiences as you lead or take part in an expedition to this place.

Word Box

expedition, journey, voyage, extreme, severe, concentrated, intense, challenging, gruelling, arduous, adrenalin, eager, thrilled, energized, thrilling

Presenting Your Work

Attach a long elastic band to your piece of writing and attach a weight to it. Then, pin the elastic band to the ceiling to make your writing look like it is on a bungee cord.

SWEET SIXTEEN

Topic	"My Super Sweet 16" is a show on MTV that takes you behind the scenes as millionaire teenagers prepare for their sixteenth birthday celebration. The show documents one character's outrageous journey as they plot, plan and prepare for a huge party. These kids expect and will only accept the absolute best.
Task	Write a story about how you prepare for your next, most outrageous millionaire birthday party.
Starters	It was one week before my _____ (number) birthday …
Guidance	• How old will you be?
	• When did you begin preparing for your birthday party?
	• Who helped you?
	• What have you arranged for?
	• What happens at the party?
Word Box	birthday, coming of age, celebration, festivity, party, event, bash, plan, arrange, set up, prepare, design, preparation, order, organize, purchase, buy
Presenting Your Work	Make an invitation for your millionaire birthday party.

the Good samaritaN

Topic	The Parable of the Good Samaritan appears in the New Testament of the Bible and tells the story of a man who is attacked, robbed and left at the side of the road. Two men walk by, but avoid him. Then, a Samaritan walks by and offers the man first aid.
Task	You are riding your bike home from a friend's place and see a poor man hungry, hurt and begging at the side of the road. He has a cardboard box in front of him that reads "Please help me!" Your parents have told you never to talk to strangers. What do you do?
Starters	Start by describing your fun, care free bike ride. Suddenly, you see the man on the side of the road…
Guidance	• What does the man look like? • Are you scared? • Do you help or do you get help? • How do you help the man? • What does the man do in return?
Word Box	help, assist, lend a hand, comfort, give food to, nourish, give to drink, miserable, heartbreaking, moving, cheerful, aid, get help, aid, good-hearted
Presenting Your Work	Make the cardboard box which the poor man has in front of him and write your story on the box.

Whodunit?

Topic	A "Whodunit" is a detective story which narrates the events of a crime. Usually, the crime is a murder. The story is told in such a way, that the identity of the criminal is not revealed until the end of the book.
Task	Write a "Whodunit." You are a famous detective who has been called to a mansion to solve a crime. None of the people present are allowed to leave the mansion until the crime is solved.
Starters	You, the famous detective, are sitting in your office when the phone suddenly rings…
Guidance	• Describe the office. • Who calls you to tell you of the crime? • What crime has been committed? • What evidence was left at the crime scene? • Who is present at the mansion? • How is the crime solved?
Word Box	crime, felony, wrongdoing, law-breaking, murder, homicide, clue, evidence, suspicion, indication, poison, weapon, suspect, mistrust, finger print, alibi
Presenting Your Work	Some detectives have a little black book in which they write all their evidence. Write your story into a little black detective book.

NiNETEEN-Eighty-four

Topic

Nineteen Eighty-Four is a classic novel by George Orwell, that was written in 1949 and that tells the story of a world where thoughts and actions are controlled by the all-seeing Big Brother. The "Thought Police" have telescreens in every household and public area, as well as hidden microphones and informers in order to catch potential criminals. Children are taught from birth to report anything suspicious.

Task

Write about what you think life would be like in a world where everything is recorded and controlled?

Starters

- Describe living in a world where everything is controlled and observed.
- Describe a typical day and how you feel.

Guidance

- How do you feel when leaving the house in the morning, knowing someone is watching you?
- As you go to school, there are cameras, microphones and police everywhere, how do you react?
- Where do you go to be alone and free?

Word Box

beliefs, feelings, opinion, view, evidence, proof, documentation, witness, control, rule, dominate, oppress, monitor, check, power, rule, surveillance

Presenting Your Work

Perhaps every person who lives in this world has a barcode. Write your story on a long piece of paper in vertical lines to make it look like a bar code.

Domestic Robot

Topic	A domestic robot is a robot used for household chores. Examples are a vacuum cleaner robot or the Korean robot "Ubiquitous" which serves drinks and meals.
Task	You have invented a new robot to help you with your every-day life. Describe your robot and what it can be used for.
Starters	You have just finished the last adjustments on your robot and are trying it out. What happens?
Guidance	• What does the robot look like? • What is the name of the robot? • What can the robot be used for? • What happens the first time you use it?
Word Box	robot, machine, contraption, device, remote control, engine, battery, obedient, disobedient , well-trained, chores, household tasks, errands, serve
Presenting Your Work	Write a computer program or code for your robot which tells it what to do. The code can look like an "html" code for example.

36   Different Places, Different Faces

Topic

Patricia Schulz's book *1000 Places to Visit Before You Die,* describes "1000 of the best places the world has to offer." In her book, Schulz describes "sacred ruins, grand hotels, wildlife reserves, hilltop villages, snack shacks, castles, festivals, reefs, restaurants, cathedrals, hidden islands, opera houses, museums and more."

Task

Write about the most interesting place you ever visited.

Starters

Think about a great place that you visited and write about what you experienced there.

Guidance

- What place did you visit?
- Where is it located?
- Describe the landscape.
- When did you visit this place?
- Who did you go with?
- What did you love about it?
- Why would you go there again?

Word Box

travel, trip, voyage, drive, ride, flight, expedition, tour, country, culture, food, sites, cuisine, places, location, climate, weather, landscape, language

Presenting Your Work

Write your text or story on a postcard. Maybe you have a picture of the place you visited. Then you can write your text on the back of the picture.

How the Elephant Got Its Wrinkles

Topic

Rudyard Kipling is a famous author who wrote *The Jungle Book* in 1894. Kipling was born in Bombay, India. In 1907, he was awarded the Nobel Prize for Literature. Kipling also wrote a story called *How the Leopard Got Its Spots*, a fictional piece, which also suggests that the Zebra got its stripes by moving "away to some little thorn-bushes where the sunlight fell all stripy, and the Giraffe moved off to some tallish trees where the shadows fell all blotchy."

Task

Write a fictional story like this one, explaining why some animals are the way they are. For example, you can write a story about how the elephant got its wrinkles.

Starters

Think of an animal that has special feature, like the elephant's wrinkles, or the toad's warts. Brainstorm ideas about how you think they might have got these features and what the animals looked like before they got them.

Guidance

I want to tell you about how the elephant got its wrinkles…

Word Box

long ago, once, some time ago, in the past, alter, transform, vary, differ, be different, contrast, diverge, turn into, become, develop into, tale, legend

Presenting Your Work

Crumble up a piece of grey card paper and straighten it out again. Repeat this two or three times, so it looks like the skin of an elephant. Then, write your text on the crumbled piece of paper.

INdiaNa JONES

Topic	*Indiana Jones and the Raiders of the Lost Ark* is an adventure film directed by Steven Spielberg in 1981. In the film, a group of ghastly soldiers is looking for an old artifact which will make their army invincible and it is up to the archeologist Indiana Jones to find it first.
Task	Write about your exciting adventure as you look for an old artifact.
Starters	What artifact are you looking for and why?
Guidance	• How old is it? • Write about why your artefact is so valuable • Where is it located? • Why is it hard to find? • Who asks you to find it? • What obstacles must you overcome to get it?
Word Box	artifact, relic, object, priceless, precious, ancient, antique, prehistoric, obsolete, adventure, quest, venture, journey, exploration, voyage, museum
Presenting Your Work	Draw a treasure map that leads you to the old artifact.

  The NObEl PriZE

Topic	On April 17, 1955, Albert Einstein died in New Jersey. Einstein was a famous physicist who discovered the theory of relativity. In 1921, Einstein won the Nobel Prize in Physics. Traditionally, the Nobel Prize is awarded for outstanding achievements in Physics, Chemistry, Literature, Peace, Medicine and Economics.
Task	You are on the Nobel Prize Committee and have been elected to invent a new prize category. What prize category do you invent and why?
Starters	I think there should be a Nobel Prize category for children in the field of…
Guidance	• What prize would you invent? Why? • Justify your new prize category. • Who would be the first person to win your prize and why?
Word Box	award, honor, appreciate, success, attainment, accomplishment, innovation, breakthrough, progress, revolution, exceptional, outstanding, excellent
Presenting Your Work	Make a certificate for your award, honoring the person who will receive it. You can also make a medal or a trophy!

The Suspicious Briefcase

Topic	Detective fiction is a type of story that centres on the investigation of a crime by a detective. Often, the crime is a murder. A famous writer of detective fiction was Agatha Christie. The Guinness Book of World Records called Christie, who lived from 1890-1967, the best selling writer of all time. She sold over one billion copies of her books in English only!
Task	As you are walking home from school, a man hands you a suspicious briefcase... Finish writing the detective story.
Starters	Describe what the man looks like and what you are thinking as he hands you the briefcase.
Guidance	• Describe the setting • Describe the man with the briefcase. • Can you open the briefcase? • What is in the briefcase? • What is suspicious about it? • What happens next?
Word Box	briefcase, piece of luggage, suspicious, dubious, shady, untrustworthy, unsafe, risky, fearful, nervous, worried, anxious, hesitant, cautious, sneaky
Presenting Your Work	Make a suitcase or briefcase out of card paper or out of a cardboard box. In it, have numbered dollar bills. Write your story on the bills and hide it under the bills.

The Magic Wand

Topic	J.K. Rowling is the author and creator of *Harry Potter*. Harry Potter is a young boy who attends Hogwarts School of Witchcraft and Wizardry. J.K. Rowling has sold over 325 million copies of her first seven Harry Potter books, which have been translated into more than 64 languages.
Task	What would you do if you had a magic wand?
Starters	Write about where you find the magic wand and how you find out that it has special powers.
Guidance	<ul><li>Where did you find the wand?</li><li>How does it work?</li><li>Where and when do you first use it?</li><li>What happens when you use it?</li><li>Will you keep the wand or store it away forever?</li></ul>
Word Box	magic, supernatural, unexplained, thrilling, magical, powerful, mystery, charm, ability, magician, mysterious, miraculous, enchanting, wizard, spell
Presenting Your Work	Make a magic wand that can be sold in a store and also make the box that it is sold in. Include a package insert which describes how the magic wand works.

The INVISIBLE MAN

Topic

The Invisible Man is a famous novel written by the English science fiction writer H.G. Wells in 1897. In it, a scientist named Griffin carries out an experiment which makes him invisible. The problem is that he can not make himself visible again!

Task

What would happen if you could become invisible whenever you wanted to? What are some of the things you could do that you cannot do now? Write a story.

Starters

Write about how you conduct the experiment that makes you invisible and the feeling you have the first time it works.

Guidance

- Describe your experiment.
- Where do you conduct your experiment?
- What happens the first time you conduct your experiment?
- What do you do as an invisible person?
- How do you become visible again?

Word Box

experiment, test, carry out, conduct, check, analysis, put to the test, invisible, unseen, undetectable, hidden, unnoticed, without being seen, disguised

Presenting Your Work

Write your story on an overhead sheet.

Dr. Jekyll and Mr. Hyde

Topic

The Strange Case of Dr. Jekyll and Mr. Hyde is a book written by the Scottish writer Robert Louis Stevenson in 1886. The story is about a London lawyer who investigates the strange case of his old friend Dr. Jekyll and the wicked Mr. Hyde. The book is well known for its portrayal of a split personality, in which at least two personalities take control of an individual's behavior.

Task

Write a story about someone who is the complete opposite of you.

Starters

- Brainstorm and write character traits about yourself on a sheet of paper.
- Write about your personality.
- What likes and dislikes do you have?
- On the opposite side of the page, write the opposite of all these traits.

Guidance

- Describe a typical day in the life of this person.
- What does he/she act like at home?
- What does he/she act like at school?
- What are his/her friends like?

Word Box

different, altered, not the same, personality, character, traits, behaviour, qualities, individuality, actions, deeds, ways, habits, hobbies, pastime, strange

Presenting Your Work

Make a big Yin and Yang symbol out of card paper. Write your story onto the symbol, using a black pen on the white part and a white pencil crayon on the black part.

Lord Of The Flies

Topic	*Lord of The Flies* was a novel written by the British writer William Golding in 1954, in which a group of school boys get stranded on a tropical island. The boys soon feel the need for a leader and vote on who that should be. One of the other boys also yearns for this position and eventually two rivalling groups fight for control over the island.
Task	Write a story about what it would be like if children ruled the world?
Starters	You can use the same scenario as William Golding uses in his novel in which the boys get stranded on the island.
Guidance	• Where have the children become stranded? • What has happened to the grown-ups? • Does anyone decide to take control? • What form of government do they establish?
Word Box	rule, govern, reign, have power over, lead, control, regime, power, leadership, government, charge, control, authority, right, permission, democracy
Presenting Your Work	Make a white rescue flag that is tied to a stick. Write your story on the flag.

The Strangest Dream

Topic

A dream is a series of images, sounds or emotions that you experience while sleeping. Sometimes dreams can seem impossible, but sometimes, they seem very realistic.

Task

Describe the strangest dream you ever had.

Starters

- Think about one of those dreams that when you woke up, you were not sure if it was real or not.
- Start by writing about yourself, going to bed and falling asleep.

Guidance

- Was there something on your mind as you were falling asleep?
- How did your dream start?
- Where did it take place?
- Who was there?
- What happened?
- Explain why your dream was so strange?

Word Box

strange, odd, bizarre, weird, out of the ordinary, peculiar, surprising, funny, perplexing, odd, curious, unexpected, remarkable, mysterious, puzzling

Presenting Your Work

Write your text or story on an old pillow case.

46

life's a fairy tale

Topic

Hans Christian Andersen was a Danish writer who lived from 1805-1875. Andersen wrote many famous fairy tales, including *The Emperor's New Clothes*, *The Snow Queen*, *The Ugly Duckling* and *The Little Mermaid*. Andersen once said: "Life itself is the most beautiful fairy tale."

Task

Write a fairy tale about a wonderful day in your life.

Starters

Keep in mind, that a fairy tale is a fictional story that usually features characters such as fairies, goblins, elves, trolls, witches, giants, talking animals and enchantments. Try to include some of these in your story.

Guidance

- Write down things that may happen in your story. Then, change it into a fairy tale.
- Use characters in your story such as fairies, goblins, elves, etc.
- Is there a moral in your story?

Word Box

charm, delight, myth, legend, magical, imaginary, legendary, make-believe, dwarves, delightful, wonderful, lovely, charming, enchanted, tale, story

Presenting Your Work

Design fancy letter paper and write your story on it. Decorate your paper with glitter, stars and sparkles.

ancient Greek Gods

Topic

The Greeks worshiped many gods. Zeus was the supreme god of the Olympians, Aphrodite was the goddess of love, Ares was the god of war, Artemis was the goddess of the hunt, Athena was the goddess of crafts and the arts, Hermes was the messenger of the gods and Poseidon was the god of the sea.

Task

You are an ancient Greek god. Describe what your day is like.

Starters

- Use the internet to look at paintings of Zeus and of some ancient Greek temples.
- Describe what they looked like.
- Describe the setting.
- Describe what you think it was like to live there.
- Do some research to make your description more realistic.

Guidance

- Which god would you choose to be? Why?
- What do you look like as a Greek god?
- What special powers do you have?
- Who are your friends and your enemies?
- What happens to you as a Greek god?

Word Box

god, Greek, Athens, power, rule, dominance, spirit, throne, rule, temple, sceptre, benign, malicious, wicked, fierce, immortal, reign, conquer, god

Presenting Your Work

Write your text on an old looking piece of paper, a wooden plank or on a white bed sheet which should represent a tunica.

HalloWEEN Horror

Topic

Halloween was originally called "Samhain", a festival among the Celts of Ireland and Great Britain. The name Halloween comes from "All Hallow's Eve", the evening before All Saints' Day. Originally, Halloween was an autumn festival which marked the end of summer. It was believed that on this evening, the dead revisited the living world, and large communal bonfires would be lit to ward off evil spirits.

Task

You and your friends are trick-or-treating at Halloween. While walking down a dark street, a person dressed up as Dracula talks to you by a bus stop. While Dracula is talking to you, you realize that his reflection does not show in the glass of the bus stop. What happens?

Starters

- Think about what costumes you and your friends are wearing.
- Describe the setting.

Guidance

- What does Dracula say to you at the bus stop?
- Who notices that his reflection does not show in the glass?
- How do you react?
- What happens next?
- How do you get out of this situation?

Word Box

celebration, Halloween, trick-or-treat, jack-o-lantern, pumpkin, scary, dark, street lights, full moon, creepy, spine-chilling, frightening, eerie, menacing

Presenting Your Work

Write your text on wax paper and make the lantern out of it.

Prime Time Boss

Topic

Ted Turner is an American media magnate. He is best known as the founder of CNN, the Cable News Network. CNN broadcasts news 24 hours a day! Ted Turner is also a philanthropist. This is someone who **donates his or her time and money** to charitable causes.

Task

You are a media magnate. What kind of TV station would you create and why?

Starters

- Think about what sort of things you like to watch on TV and make a list of them.
- Also, think about other programming that you would like to broadcast, like documentaries, arts & crafts, music & entertainment, comedy, film, etc.

Guidance

- What kind of TV station would you create?
- What shows would you broadcast and why?
- How do you convince your team that these programs are the right ones to send?

Word Box

television, TV, broadcast, air, show, televise, put on air, make known, prime time, commercial, advertising, magnate, mogul, entrepreneur, broadcasting

Presenting Your Work

Make a TV programme for the whole week, showing only the things you like to watch.

The Perfect Blizzard

Topic

A massive snowstorm with very low temperatures, strong winds and heavy blowing snow is known as a blizzard. A blizzard in 1995 brought meters of snow and temperatures of below -30°C to Minnesota. The blizzard caused almost $82 million in damage and 11 counties in southern Minnesota were declared federal disaster areas.

Task

Make up a story about yourself as you are stuck in this blizzard.

Starters

Describe the setting to a person who has never seen snow.

Guidance

- Describe what the snow looks and feels like.
- What does the cold feel like in your face when you step outside?
- What is it like to walk through the deep snow?
- How did you get stuck in the blizzard?
- How do you get out of the situation?

Word Box

blizzard, snowstorm, wind, blustery weather, twist, coil, chilly, freezing, icy, bitter, arctic, frost, pain, ache, throbbing, hard to breathe, inhale, blistering

Presenting Your Work

Make a snow globe to go with your writing by attaching a small figurine to the bottom of a baby food jar and filing it with water (to about 1cm from the top). Then, add silver glitter, close the lid and make it water tight by using a glue gun.

Sample Lesson

Topic
Back to the
Future (Prompt 9)

In 1985, Amblin Entertainment released the movie *Back to the Future*. The movie is about a crazy scientist, Doc Brown, who makes a time machine out of a fancy sports car. Doc's young friend Marty McFly, a typical American teenager, is accidentally sent back to 1955 and has to find a way to get back home.

Start with a Bang!

Starting out with a bang is the most vital part of the lesson. Writing should be taught with emotion and fire and it is essential to stimulate young writers right from the beginning. Students love to hear or see exciting and hard-to-believe facts, figures and images about their writing topic, so give them what they want to see.

I start this one out by showing the students a time machine that I have built out of a cardboard box and taped to a seat. I ask them what they think it is. Then, I show them how it works.

Vocabulary

Next, I do some vocabulary work by asking the students to tell me some words that have to do with time travel. I try to incorporate all the words in the Word Box. These are all defined (as a class) and written on the board.

Word Box

time-travel, era, period, hyperspace, past, yesteryear, forthcoming, future, eager, wound-up, swift, like a flash, astounded, stunned, Milky Way, universe

If you want to do more work on vocabulary, you can play a "Definition

Game" in which the kids must match strips of paper. One strip has the word; the other strip has the definition. An example is provided hereinafter.

| A picture in your mind | Now give the students the chance to develop a picture in their minds about their topic. I give them about twenty minutes to draw their time machine. I tell them to add all the gadgets and tools that make their machine work. When they are finished, I ask them to describe their machine (in writing) and how it works. |

I always have the students write double-spaced. That way, when they are editing, they can make notes and corrections between the lines.

Guidance	• What does your time machine look like?
	• What is special about it?
	• How does it work?

Now I show the students a short clip of the 1985 movie *Back to the Future,* when Doc Brown explains his invention to Marty and Marty uses it the first time. If students are having trouble getting started, you may want to show the clip before the students start drawing their time machine.

| Research | Next, the students should think about a period in time that they would like to visit and research this. Have them use the class library or the internet. If they want to visit the Middle Ages, they should find out how people lived and what they wore. This is done to make their writing more realistic. Give them a list of guiding questions. Also, at this point, show them (but do not hand out) the Writing Checklist hereinafter, so the students are aware of the stages they will go through in their writing process. |

Guidance
- Where do you go on your first trip?
- What was life like at the time?
- What do you think life will be like at this time?
- What do/did people wear?
- How did/will they live?
- Which famous person would you visit? Why?
- What would you ask him/her?

Story Sequence

After that, the students should write a short summary of what will happen in their story by using the "Story Sequence" template hereinafter. They have already done the first step of this by answering some of the guiding questions, but at this point, it is important for them to put their events in order. This will give their writing more structure. I allow students to do this in point form.

First Draft

Now the students can write their first draft by adding detail to the summary they have written. It is worthwhile to have the children make sketches while they write. This helps them to create an image in their minds of what people, places and things look like.

Peer Editing

The students should read their story to a friend. The friend should give feedback by asking questions and making comments like "I didn't quite understand this!" or "I think you may have made a mistake here!"

The student who has written the piece should make notes on post-it notes and make adjustments to his/her writing. You can also have the students read their work in front of the class. This is more time consuming, but you have more command over the feedback sessions. This way, the teacher can also give feedback.

Draft 2	The students should now make changes to their writing by adding the information from the peer-editing session. Before handing in the final draft, the students should fill out the "Writing Checklist" hereinafter, to make sure that no steps were left out.
Hand-in	After the "Writing Checklist" has been filled out and adjustments have been made, the students should hand in their stories. At this point, the teacher corrects the paper for spelling, grammar and coherence.
Draft 3 or Final Draft	If you are satisfied with the content of the writing, have the students write their final draft. You can use the template in this book for doing so, which allows the children to illustrate their writing. If the writing still needs additions or more work, have the students write a third draft to add more detail. Remind them that in order to produce a great piece of writing, they will need persistence. Hemingway rewrote *A Farewell to Arms* thirty times before having it published!
Score Your Writing	When the students have completed their final draft, it is time for them to score their writing. Celebrate the hard work and effort they put into their work.
	Then, have the children score their writing on the template hereinafter. I go through this with the students step-by-step, to ensure that they understand every sentence and all the concepts.
	Finally, have the students hand in their scoring sheets. Review the scoring sheets and tick off where you think the student should be placed. You can then hand the sheets back or, what is even more effective, review it with each student. This can be done during a silent reading session for example.

Definition Game

Match the words with the appropriate definitions

time-travel	To be completely surprised.
period	A synonym for period.
hyperspace	Being very enthusiastic or anxious to do something.
past	Moving backwards or forwards to different points in time.
era	Very fast.
eager	A synonym for swift.
swift	An interval of time that an event or chain of events takes place within.
astounded	A concept of time. These events have not yet happened.
stunned	A synonym for eager.
forthcoming	An event that has yet to occur.
like a flash	A synonym for astounded.
wound-up	A portion or event in time that has already occurred.
future	In the past.
yesteryear	A term often used in science fiction writing to describe an extremely fast way of travelling.

Name: _____

Definition Game

Match the words with the appropriate definitions

Name: _____

Writing Checklist

Prewriting
- [ ] Select your topic.
- [ ] Write questions or brainstorm about your topic.
- [ ] Research your topic.
- [ ] Planning Your Writing: Write a story sequence.

Your First Draft
- [ ] Beginning: Introduce your topic (What will you write about?)
- [ ] Middle: Answer all the questions you have written down in the prewriting stage.
- [ ] End: End with an important thought or idea about your topic.

Revision
- [ ] Read your first draft and check for mistakes.
- [ ] Peer Editing: Have a friend review your story. Have them write down any questions they may have about the story.
- [ ] Make changes and answer all the additional questions.

Editing
- [ ] Check for errors.
- [ ] Have someone else check for errors.
- [ ] Plan and write your final draft.

Final Draft
- [ ] Give your best to present your final draft. Make illustrations to go with your writing.

Name: _____

Story SEQUENCE

In the beginning, _____

_____

_____

_____

Then, _____

_____

_____

_____

After that, _____

_____

_____

_____

Next, _____

_____

_____

_____

In the end, _____

_____

_____

_____

NAME: _____

SCORE YOUR WRITING

Check the box that you think best fits to your piece of writing. Then, have your teacher read your work and check the boxes. Have you chosen the same boxes? Why? Why not?

VG = very good   G = good   NW = needs work

		VG	G	NW
Writing Process	I have planned my writing effectively, by brainstorming and/or writing down what will happen in my story.	☐	☐	☐
	My story has a clear beginning, middle and end.	☐	☐	☐
	My beginning grabs the reader's attention and gives clues about what will happen in my story.	☐	☐	☐
	Every detail in my story adds a little bit more to the main idea.	☐	☐	☐
	I have revised my story by adding as many interesting details as possible to make it more interesting.	☐	☐	☐
	I have edited my story by reading through it to find mistakes.	☐	☐	☐
	I ended my story with an exciting or unexpected twist. I have a strong conclusion or ending.	☐	☐	☐
Voice	My writing has personality. It sounds different from the way others write.	☐	☐	☐
	I have included important thoughts and feelings into my writing and the reader will know how I feel.	☐	☐	☐
	I have confidence in my writing and feel comfortable about sharing it with others.	☐	☐	☐
	I have given a lot of thought to who my audience is and the readers know that I am talking to them through my writing.	☐	☐	☐

Name: _____

		VG	G	NW

Ideas & Content

The topic is fully developed and grabs the reader's attention. ☐ ☐ ☐

I know a lot about this topic and have added interesting information. ☐ ☐ ☐

I wrote about what is happening in my story, instead of "telling." ☐ ☐ ☐

I can easily answer the question "What is my story about?" ☐ ☐ ☐

Word Choice

I have used colorful, exciting words in my writing. ☐ ☐ ☐

I have tried to include some new vocabulary in my writing to add to the main idea or topic. ☐ ☐ ☐

I have used energetic adjectives and verbs to make my story more exciting. ☐ ☐ ☐

I have used such good words that the reader won't soon forget them. ☐ ☐ ☐

Spelling

I have re-read my writing to find spelling mistakes. ☐ ☐ ☐

I have used capitals correctly. ☐ ☐ ☐

Every paragraph in my writing shows where a new idea begins. ☐ ☐ ☐

Periods, commas, exclamations marks, quotation marks and question marks are in the right place. ☐ ☐ ☐

Sentences

I have varied the length of my sentences. Some are long and attention-grabbing, some are short and exciting. ☐ ☐ ☐

My story is easy and fun to read out loud. It sounds great! ☐ ☐ ☐

My sentences all begin differently. ☐ ☐ ☐

I have re-read my story to cut out or change sentences that do not belong or are uninteresting. ☐ ☐ ☐

What areas do you think you did really well in writing this piece? What areas need improvement?

....

....

....

Name:

Write like Your Hands are on Fire
By Stefan Czarnecki

Out Now!

Write like Your Hands are on Fire

A Collection of Effective Report Card Comments

Student Profiles

INQUIRER

- shows natural curiosity
- has acquired the skills necessary to conduct purposeful, constructive research

Adjectives
inquisitive – inquiring – curious – interested – involved – analytical – fascinated – captivated – engagedshows natural curiosity

THINKER

- exercises initiative in applying thinking skills critically and creatively
- makes sound decisions

Adjectives
thinker – analytical – investigative – systematic – methodical – rational – exploratory – critical – efficient

COMMUNICATOR

- receives and expresses ideas and information confidently

Adjectives
expressive – communicative – outgoing – approachable – amicable – good-natured – agreeable – kind

RISK-TAKER

- approaches unfamiliar situations without anxiety
- has the confidence and independence of spirit to explore new roles, ideas and strategies
- is courageous and articulate in defending those things in which he/she believes

Adjectives
confident – independent – articulate – courageous – self-assured – self-confident – assertive – poised – self-regulating – self-sufficient – self-reliant – eloquent – fluent

KNOWLEDGEABLE

- spends school time exploring themes which have global relevance and importance
- acquires a critical mass of significant knowledge

Adjectives
knowledgeable – well-informed – on the ball – informed – well-read – clued-in – alert – sharp – ready to act

Other Books By Stefan Czarnecki

Look for these titles out soon!

Write Like Your Hands are on Fire Series:

Write Like Your Hands are on Fire

Kids Poetry Slam - Writing and Presenting Remarkable Poems

Write Like Your Hands are on Fire

50 Kreative Schreibanlässe für den Englischunterricht

Outdoor adventure

The Ultimate Guide to Fun Outside!

LaVergne, TN USA
18 January 2011
212971LV00005B/148/P